BEYOND THE FRINGE

BEYOND THE FRINGE

by Alan Bennett
Peter Cook
Jonathan Miller
Dudley Moore

RANDOM HOUSE · NEW YORK

Beyond the Fringe *opened in London at the Fortune Theatre, on May 10, 1961, under the auspices of William Donaldson and Donald Albery. It was first presented in New York by Alexander H. Cohen, at the John Golden Theatre, on October 27, 1962, with the following cast:*

ALAN BENNETT

PETER COOK

JONATHAN MILLER

DUDLEY MOORE

Original London Production Directed by Eleanor Fazan
Setting by John Wyckham
Lighting by Ralph Alswang
Production Associates: André Goulston and Gabriel Katzka

PART ONE

PART TWO

BEYOND THE FRINGE

Part One

STEPPES IN THE RIGHT DIRECTION

JONATHAN, PETER and ALAN are sitting or standing around the stage as the curtain rises.

DUDLEY enters through the arch, walks to the piano, and sits down and plays the National Anthem. The other THREE all stand. After the National Anthem, DUDLEY exits and the other THREE all sit down again.

PETER

Who is that fellow who keeps coming in and playing "God Save the Queen"?

JON

I don't know, but he's not English. No Englishman would keep coming in and keep playing the National Anthem quite like that.

ALAN

He's not English, certainly.

PETER

Do you know what I think he is?

JON

No, what do you think he is?

PETER

I think he is a member of the Moscow State Circus.

JON

Really, what makes you say that?

PETER

Well, I was in the washroom the other day and I was chatting to him—he was developing some photographs or something at the time—and I asked what he was doing over here, and he said, "I am a member of the Moscow State Circus." So I put two and two together. The whole thing added up to his being a member . . .

ALL

. . . of the Moscow State Circus.

ALAN

He's an awfully nice fellow.

ALL

Awfully nice fellow!

ALAN

But I do wish he wouldn't keep coming in and playing "God Save the Queen."

JON

I quite agree with you—I mean I like the National Anthem. I like to start the day with the National Anthem.

4

PETER

Exactly, but every other minute of the day—I prefer a more sedentary way of life, myself.

ALAN

It's probably because they get so very little chance to play it over there.

JON

It's amazing how little their Bolshevism has contaminated their music.

PETER

Practically not at all—they play like absolute angels.

JON and ALAN

Absolute angels. Absolute Engels.

PETER

We could do with some of them over here.

ALL

Oh, we could, indeed.

PETER

I tell you what, next time he comes in why don't we grab him, and try and indoctrinate him—win him over to our point of view. Jonathan, you lie doggo behind there. Alan, you lull his suspicions, look fat and contented—symbolize the British way of life. And I'll be behind this hat stand here. Cavey, chaps, here he comes. (DUDLEY *enters through the arch. He sees* PETER, *who pretends to be dusting the hat stand.* Hello, there's a bit of dust on this hat stand I was just . . .

5

BEYOND THE FRINGE

(DUDLEY *gets to the steps and they all rush forward and grab him*) Right ... Hello, there. Sit down, we're quite friendly—welcome to our lovely land, we hope you'll be very happy. No need to be alarmed.

ALAN

You'll have to shout at him—they don't speak a word of English.

PETER

We in this country enjoy a high standard of living, with a considerable measure of political freedom—

ALAN

Under the National Health Service for twelve shillings a week we are treated absolutely free.

PETER

Having any effect?

JON

No, he's quite impervious. We'll have to try shock tactics.

PETER

Shock tactics—what do you suggest? (*They whisper together*) Oh, yes. (*To* DUDLEY:) Hello there, Russian man. Now, you listen to me—I'm going to say something that will change your whole ideology. Just you listen to me. Khrushchev—*ssss* (*Bronx cheer*).

JON

All right, all together. Khrushchev—ssss, Khrushchev—ssss. No, it's no good. It's not positive enough.

ALAN

It's too negative?

JON

Far too negative. Why not offer him something positive
from our own culture—something encouraging from our way
of life to persuade him to join us.

PETER

Yes—what have we got? I know—trump card! Now you
listen again, Russian man. I want you to say after me these
words—it's quite simple. Macmillan—mmmm. Now you have
a shot. It's good fun. Macmillan—mmmm . . .

DUDLEY
(*Simultaneously*)

. . . ssss.

PETER

No, you're quite wrong, it's Khrushchev—ssss, it's Macmillan—mmmm.

DUDLEY
(*Simultaneously*)

. . . ssss.

PETER

Macmillan—mmmm.

DUDLEY
(*Simultaneously*)

. . . ssss.

PETER

Macmillan—mmmm. Smile, you stupid Serbo-Croat!

ALAN

No, no, it's no use. Macmillan's obviously too bitter a pill to swallow first time.

JON

All right. Let's start with something harmless or innocuous that he can't possibly take exception to, like Lord Snowden, and work slowly up into a climax and hit him with it.

PETER

All right, you set the ball rolling, would you?

JON

Yes. Right, then. Something really fatuous to begin with. C. P. Snow—mmmm.

ALAN

Rule Britannia—mmmm.

PETER

Arnold Wesker—mmmm.

JON

Henley Regatta—mmmm.

ALAN

Abide With Me—mmmm.

PETER

This sea-girt isle—mmmm.

JON

Ian Fleming—mmmm.

ALAN

T. S. Eliot—mmmm.

PETER

Robin Hood—mmmm.

JON

Never had it . . .

ALAN

. . . so good—

ALL

Macmillan—mmmm.

DUDLEY
(*Simultaneously*)

. . . ssss.

PETER

No—you don't seem to understand at all. It's Khrushchev—ssss. It's Macmillan—mmmm.

DUDLEY
(*Simultaneously*)

. . . ssss.

PETER

No, Macmillan—mmmm.

DUDLEY
(*Simultaneously*)

. . . ssss.

PETER

Macmillan—ssss— Do you know, I think he's got something—

JON

Macmillan—ssss. Macmillan—ssss. Well, I must admit it's got a certain lilt to it.

ALAN

Macmillan—ssss. It's short but it's catchy.

ALL
(*Singing*)

Macmillan—ssss.
Macmillan—ssss.
    (DUDLEY *playing the "Volga Boatmen"*)
Macmillan—ssss.
Macmillan—*hoy!*

Blackout

ROYAL BOX

PETER

No, I won't have a program, thank you very much. Excuse me, is this P. Row P?

DUDLEY

Yes, P 1, 2, and 3.

PETER

I'm P 3.

DUDLEY

I'm P 2.

PETER

I'm most frightfully sorry to come in late like this but I couldn't get a taxi, you know how it is at this time of night.

DUDLEY

Oh yes, I know how it is. Well, you've only missed three and a half minutes of the overture. It's a seven-and-a-half-minute overture actually.

PETER

You've seen this show before, have you?

DUDLEY

Oh yes, I've seen this show, let me see now, five hundred—no, I tell a lie—four hundred and ninety-seven times.

PETER

Four hundred ninety-seven times. That must be some sort of a record. Are you that fond of the show?

DUDLEY

Oh no. It's not my sort of show at all, really.

PETER

Well, why on earth do you keep coming?

DUDLEY

Well, you see, it's the Royal Family.

PETER

The Royal Family? Are they in some way connected—

DUDLEY

No. No, you see, I read in the newspapers that the Royal Family was planning a visit to this theatre, so naturally I came along. You see, up there, that's what they call the Royal Box. But I don't know if you've noticed, there's no Royalty in it. No Royal People there at all. No Royal Personage actually gracing the Royal Box . . . unless of course they're crouching. But, I mean, that wouldn't be Royalty, would it?

PETER

Not crouching, no.

DUDLEY

No, not on the crouch.

PETER

Not on the crouch, they don't go in for that very much.

DUDLEY

Anyway, I was here last Tuesday and guess who I saw.

PETER

Do you really want me to guess?

DUDLEY

Yes, go on, guess.

PETER

Arthur Tinty.

DUDLEY

Arthur Tinty!

PETER

It's just a guess. He sometimes comes to the theatre.

DUDLEY

Arthur Tinty. No, I can't say I saw Arthur Tinty.

PETER

Well, he probably wasn't here.

DUDLEY

I tell you who I did see, Arthur Grodes, but I can't say I saw Arthur Tinty.

PETER

Well, don't worry—he may not have been here.

DUDLEY

No, what's he look like?

PETER

Tinty, well, he's very hard to describe, really. He has a typical Tinty look about him. Average height. Average build.

DUDLEY

I saw him. Yes—so that's Arthur Tinty. But is he regal?

PETER

No, he's not regal, no.

DUDLEY

Noble?

PETER

Not noble, no.

DUDLEY

No, well, er— Anyway, I am hoping against hope that one night the Royal Family will turn up and make my having to sit through this rotten, awful show every night worth while.

PETER

Do your really mean to say you spend fifteen shillings every night just on the off-chance you may catch a glimpse of the Royal Family?

DUDLEY

Well, they're not worth the pound.

Blackout

MAN BITES GOD

JON
(In dimness. On mike)

The time is seven o'clock! By the Grace of God and Associated Rediffusion, we bring you "Always on a Sunday"! A program of religion on the move. Let there be light!

(The light goes on)

DUDLEY
(Singing)

If your baby does you wrong,
Turn the other cheek.
Keep it turning, turning, turning.
Love thy neighbor as thyself,
Turn the other cheek.

Now if the Lord starts getting stroppy,
Don't think you are soppy
If you turn the other cheek.
Oh, keep it turning, turning, turning . . .

JON

Thank you. Jolly good, boys. Thank you very much. That was really spiffing. It really had my feet tapping. Now let's get down to God. God. Who is He, where is He, and above all, why is He—and of course why is He above all? Now, Dudley, have you got any questions you would like to fire off about God?

DUDLEY

Yes . . . well, Vicar . . .

JON

Don't call me Vicar—call me Dick—that's the sort of Vicar I am!

DUDLEY

Well, Dicker . . . one thing that has always been a great mystery to me is the exact age of the Almighty. How old is God?

JON

Good, good! Good God! Well, Dudley—it isn't really a question of age with God. You see, God is ageless. That is to say, He's age-old. He's old-aged, if you like. In fact, God is as old as He feels and in that way He's exactly the same as you or I and that's the message I'm trying to get across to you youngsters down at my little dockland parish of St. Jack in the Lifeboat. You see, I think we have got to get right away from this stuffy old idea of thinking of God as something holy or divine, and once we do that we'll get you youngsters flooding back into the churches—I know that for sure. Now—Alan—is there anything in the Bible that actually puts you off religion?

ALAN

Well, I'm glad you asked that.

} together

DUDLEY

Thank you. Allan, do you mind, do you mind?

DUDLEY

Thank you, Alan—can we leave Lot's wife till later? Well, Dicker, during my study of the good work I was very shocked by all the cruelty and violence in the New Testament. I mean, take for example this ghastly case of shoving a needle up the eye of a camel. Now that's taking unfair advantage of a dumb animal. It's an appalling sight, the poor old ship of the desert standing there with a needle up his eye—and frankly, Dicker, that was the straw that broke the camel's back.

ALL

Last straw.

JON

Yes, thank you, yes. Well, I think you are putting words into God's mouth here, and I think we can turn a blind eye on the whole affair—after all, the camel had to, by Jove, yes. But I am very grateful to you, Dudley, for bringing this up, because it does bring me to the whole problem of juvenile violence in general. Now I think an awful lot of tommyrot has been spoken about teen-age and juvenile violence. I think we can use this violence and channel it towards God. It is my aim to get the violence off the streets and into the churches, where it belongs. In the old days people used to think of the saints as pious old milksops—well, they weren't. The old saints were rough, toothless—no, I mean tough, ruthless tearaways who knew where they were going. Matthew, Mark, Luke and John went through life with their heads screwed on. That's the little rhyme we all sing—and with these principles firmly in mind, we've now got ourselves a young, vigorous church where youngsters like yourselves can come in off the streets, pick up a chick, jive in the aisles, and really have yourselves a ball. The result is we are playing to packed houses every night, except of course for Sunday, when we are forced to close our doors because of the Lord's Day Observance Society.

Blackout

FRUITS OF EXPERIENCE

ALAN BENNETT SOLO

We're going to have just a little chat this evening about international relations. I'd like to kick off, if I may, by quoting you something said by H. R. H. The Duke of Edinburgh, God bless him, to the Annual General Meeting of the World Federation of Women's Institutes. He said, and I quote here: "So far as Anglo-American relations are concerned . . ." (Laughter) ". . . I am not an expert, but I am going to stick my neck right out and say that our two great countries, that's to say Great Britain and America, ought to get together." Now, I think in his own inimitable fashion His Royal Highness has put his finger on it. It's tremendously important that we in Great Britain should try and pass on to you in America some of that traditional wisdom and experience which has come down to us, from hand to mouth, from generation to generation.

And I think the first thing you've got to learn is that this business of international politics is a game. It's a game. To start with, there are two sides . . . I've no need to tell you who they are . . . It's a hard game, it's a rough game . . . sometimes alas, it's a dirty game, but the point about a game, surely, is that there's no need to take it seriously. Anyway, that's what we in Great Britain think and we've been playing the game now for rather a long time. Give a year, take a year—a thousand years. And in our day you see we were a bloody good side. Bloody good side. And we still are. Oh yes. But naturally—well, we're a bit long in the tooth, a bit short in the wind. But that's where *you* come in, you see. Because you've only just come onto the field . . . you're young, you're vigorous, you're alive . . . of course you're a bit raw, you've got a bit more brawn than brains . . . but that's where *we* come in, you see. Together, together we're world beaters.

Now, let's try and find out where it is that you've been going wrong. Take all that Cuban business . . . oh dear, oh dear, oh dear. No no no no. Of course, one can see what you were trying to do . . . trying, I suppose, in your own way to emulate our splendid effort at Suez. Ah well, you'll live and learn.

Now, before I go I would like to set your mind at rest on one point. While I've been over here in your charming country several people have come up to me and said, "Now look here, old chap, where does Great Britain stand in the nuclear defense pogr—program, sorry." Well, I can reassure you on this point—we are all very much of one mind on nuclear defense. Wouldn't like you to take any notice of these Ban the Bombers. You know Bertrand Russell and hooligans like that, sincere though these people are, I mean I yield to no one in my admiration for Bertrand Russell. He's a great philosopher and nudist. But as a thinker, as a thinker he should stick to thinking—he shouldn't meddle in politics. After all, we live in a democracy. Government isn't run by people like that. It's run by the people. Of course, I suppose he's right in this sense that the hydrogen bomb is a terrible weapon. It *is*. I know it kills millions of people, I know it seals the fate of millions as yet unborn. All right.

Fair enough. But I put this to you. The hydrogen bomb is just the same as the bow and arrow in principle . . . and thank goodness, in this modern world today, our two great countries care about principles.

Blackout

BOLLARD

ALAN *is on the rostrum with a camera.* JON *and* PETER *enter.*

JON

So I said to him, I said, "Do you do vests in mauve?" And he said, "No, we don't do vests in mauve." "Don't do vests in mauve," I said very sharply. "No," he said. So I had to settle for the green, the Lincoln green!

PETER

I think you look lovely in green, you look like a tree lizard.

JON

Hello, Arthur, what have we got today?

ALAN

Surprise! Surprise! Today we've got Bollard.

JON

Bollard? That sounds exciting. What is it?

ALAN

It's a ciggy.

PETER

Oh, a cigarette.

20

DUDLEY

(*Entering*)

Hello, men! So sorry I'm late, I got held up at the hair-dresser's. I was so worried about it, I can't tell you. He was going on and on—I said, "Stop, you'll ruin it!"

JON

No, he hasn't.

DUDLEY

What's the back like?

PETER

Lovely, lovely. You can hardly see the join.

DUDLEY

Thank you. (*Bumps into* JON) Oh, hello— Oh, have you seen what I've seen? Oh, Cyril, what a lovely tie you're sporting!

PETER

It is a lovely tie. It's the new color.

DUDLEY

Qu'est que c'est, gue ça? Well, what is it?

PETER

Blue. Can't you see?

DUDLEY

Oh, I say, aren't these sou'-westers fabulous?

ALAN

Come along, then.
    (*They move to top. They group.* ALAN *poses* DUDLEY)

DUDLEY

Oh, please don't touch me this morning, Arthur.

ALAN

Oh. Are you ready? Right! Action!

DUDLEY

Stormy days at sea are followed

PETER

By the smoking of a Bollard.

JON

Once that lovely smoke is swallowed,
so much Satisfaction!
Smoke Bollard—a man's cigarette.

ALL

Whoops!

Blackout

THE HEAT DEATH OF THE UNIVERSE

JONATHAN MILLER SOLO

Some years ago, when I was rather hard up, I wanted to buy myself a new pair of trousers—but being hard up, I could not afford to buy a new pair. However, some kind friend told me that if I looked sharp about it I could get myself a very nice second-hand pair from the Sales Department of the London Passenger Transport Board Lost Property. Now before I accepted this interesting offer I got involved in a certain amount of fastidious conflict with my inner soul as I was not very keen to assume the trousers which some lunatic had taken off on a train going eastbound towards Whitechapel.

However, after a certain amount of moral contortion in this area, I managed to steel myself to the alien crutch, and made my way towards the shop in question, praying as I did so, "Oh, God, let them be dry-cleaned when I get there." And when I arrived there, you can imagine my pleasure and surprise when I found, instead of a disheveled heap of lunatics' trousers lying all over the place, a very neat heap of brand-new, bright blue corduroy trousers. There were four hundred of them. How can anyone lose four hundred pairs of trousers on a train? I mean, it's hard enough to lose a brown paper bag full of old orange peel when you really try very hard. Besides which, four hundred men wearing no trousers in the rush hour— No, it's obviously part of a London

23

Passenger Transport Board plot—a rather complex economic scheme along Galbraithian or Keynesian lines—something rather baroque to expand the economy. So we go over to investigate this to the London Passenger Transport Board Economics Planning Division Ops Room. "Carry on smoking. Operation Cerulean Trousers. Now we are going to issue each one of you men a brand-new, bright blue pair of corduroy trousers. Your job will be to spread out to all parts of London, to empty railway carriages, and there in the darkness and solitude you are to divest yourselves of these garments and leave them in horrid little heaps on the floors of the carriages concerned. Do I make myself absolutely clear? Good—well, on your way. Godspeed, chins up and trousers down!"

Then out into the blue of the night the four hundred men disperse identically in blue corduroy trousers, trying to look as inconspicuous as a great massed phalanx of four hundred men dressed in identical blue corduroy trousers possibly can look. And they disperse to places far out on the ends of the central line, places out on the Essex marshes, which are totally uninhabited, one presumes, except for a few stray wading marsh birds mournfully pacing the primeval slime.

And there in the moonlit sidings they let themselves separately and individually into the empty compartments and just before the final awful existential act of detrouserment they do some of those things people sometimes do in railway compartments when they think they are alone . . . or, indeed, alone anywhere for that matter. Things like . . . well, things like smelling their own armpits.

Of course, it's quite possible the men did not remove their trousers in the compartments at all but with a proper sense of privacy made their way along the corridor to the locked seclusion of the lavatory. Now English Railway lavatories have a rather mysterious, unpunctuated motto printed on the wall, saying, "Gentlemen lift the seat." Now, what exactly does this mean? It could be a blunt military order—it might be an invitation to upper-class larceny—

Anyway, one way or the other, off come the trousers and then the four hundred half-naked men make their way back to headquarters through the sleeping chilly streets of nocturnal London—four hundred fleet white nude figures in the night, their eight hundred horny feet pattering on the pavements and arousing small children from their slumbers in upstairs bedrooms. Children who are soothed back into their sleep by their parents with the ancient words, "Turn your face to the wall, my darling, while the gentlemen trot by."

Blackout

DEUTSCHER CHANSONS

JON

And now Dudley Moore accompanies himself upon the pianoforte in settings of European songs. First a setting by Fauré of Verlaine's poem, *"La nuit s'épanouit,"* in which the poet bemoans the evil spirits which are at the bottom of his garden. *"La nuit s'épanouit."*

DUDLEY
(*Sings*)

La nuit s'épanouit dans la vie sanglotante
Et les ombres velours des vagues ténèbreuses
S'en vont dans les bonnes de la vague distance
Sanglotant violon sanglotant
Sanglotant violon sanglotant de l'amour.

JON

And now Dudley Moore continues to play with himself, this time in a setting by Schubert of Heiner's poem, *"Die Flabbergast,"* in which the poet and his lover bemoan, and bemoan, and bemoan *"Die Flabbergast."*

26

BEYOND THE FRINGE

DUDLEY
(Sings)

Ist eine hünst die far die Flabbergast
Ist Sweinhunst die fi hein heinst.
Ist eine hünst die far die Flabbergast
Ist Sweinhunst die fi hein heinst.
Finish is "Ist mein
Ist mein."

Blackout

THE SADDER AND WISER
BEAVER

ALAN *and* PETER *come through the archway.*

ALAN

And you're still working for Beaverbrook?

PETER

Well yes, I'm still working for the Beaver, if work's the right word. Don't get me wrong, Alan, I haven't changed, working on the paper hasn't altered my outlook. You and I in the old days always used to think alike on most things. Well, it's just the same now—you name any issue and I'll agree with you on it.

Just because my name's at the top of the column you mustn't think I have any connection with it, it's just that I think he does a grand job of work, and if ever I have to write anything on him, every now and then I am forced to write something. I always ring him up afterwards and apologize, or get my secretary to. You've met the wife, got a lovely little house now down in East Grinstead, two little kids, you've got to fight for it. We go for holidays in Germany, drink a stein with the people, I like the people.

I'm working on the novel, you know. One day that novel's going to come out and blast the lid off the whole filthy business—name the names, show up Fleet Street for what it really is—a really accurate novel about all those people. But if you are going to write a really accurate novel, you've got to join the people you are writing about for a while anyway. I am going through a sort of research period at the moment.

There are about ten of us on the paper, young, progressive liberal people who don't believe a word we are writing, and whenever the old man has a party—a cocktail party—we all gather together down the far end of the room, and drink as much as we can—we really knock it back—we drink and drink and drink—trying to break him from within; then—quite openly, behind our hands—we snigger at him.

ALAN

You snigger at him?

PETER

That's right! We snigger and titter at him, "Ha ha, putting on a bit of weight in St. Tropez."

ALAN

Well, I don't know, it doesn't seem very much to me—sniggering and tittering.

PETER

A titter here, a titter there—it all adds up—you'd be surprised—

ALAN

Well, take me—I'm no saint, but I turned down five thousand pounds a year with an advertising agency, because I didn't want to make that sort of money.

BEYOND THE FRINGE

PETER

Yes, I think that is wonderful of you, Alan, really wonderful—in a way I wish I could be like you. But we don't all come into fifty thousand pounds at the age of twenty-one.

Blackout

WORDS . . . AND THINGS

ALAN

Hello there, Urchfont, how are you?

JON

Hello there, Bleaney.

ALAN

Hello— What was that little philosophical paper you were telling me about in Common Room—Hegel's Moral Doubts, I think you said it was.

JON

Oh, that—well, it's not really a paper so much as an annotation which I've run up for the proceedings of the Aristotelian Society. It's certainly no principia—shall I fire ahead?

(DUDLEY *walks on, then exits*)

ALAN

Oh yes.

JON

Now Wittgenstein says, does he not, rather ham-handedly in my opinion, in the Blue and Brown books, that the statement, "Fetch me that slab," implies there is a slab, such that were I to fetch it, the statement, "Fetch me that slab," would be disjunctively denied by the opposite statement.

ALAN

Yes.

JON

Well, it seems to me Wittgenstein has made rather a bad blunder here, for as far as I can see, the unfetched slab can claim to exist really no more than the unseen tree in the quad.

ALAN

No no, I think you're making a rather primitive category mistake here.

JON

Surely not.

ALAN

Oh no, you're not, it's me. I'm terribly sorry.

JON

No no no, it seems to me what we have here is an example of a synthetic a-priori proposition of the sort "there are no sense data which are both blue and green all over at the same time and sense data," which is a statement really both about our world as we know it in the Wittgenstein sense of everything that is the case, and also a statement about our language as we use it. Now, I know you get very worked up about propositional disjunctive functions, Bleaney, so I thought you might like to deal with the whole . . .

ALAN

Yes.

JON

I see. Well, tell me—are you using yes in its affirmative sense here?

ALAN

No no. I like that paper. I liked it, you see, because it bears on something I am considering myself, namely, what part—what role—we as philosophers play in this great heterogeneous - confusing - and - confused - jumble - of - political - social - and - economic - relationships - we - call - Society. I mean, other people have jobs to do, don't they—what do people do these days?

JON

They chop down trees.

ALAN

They chop down trees, they drive buses, or they play games.

JON

Yes, that's very important—they play games.

ALAN

Now, we also play games, but we as philosophers play language games. Games at language. Now, when you and I go onto the cricket pitch, we do so secure in the knowledge that a game of cricket is in the offing. But when we play language games, we do so rather in order to find out what game it is we are playing. In other words, why do we do philosophy at all? Why?

JON

Why yes, why yes . . . no no. I think I must take exception with you on that point, Bleaney, for it seems we want to ask not so much why questions as how questions.

ALAN

Why?

JON

Well, there you are—need I say more?

ALAN

Yes.

JON

Well, I shall. It seems to me that philosophers, or at least they like to call themselves philosophers, who start off by asking why questions end up by making pseudo statements of the sort . . . Saturday got into bed with me . . .

ALAN

Is that a pseudo statement?

JON

Well, I'll take one from real life . . . in that case, hammer home the point . . . there is too much Tuesday in my beetroot salad, or something of that general sort.

ALAN

I think that is perfectly obvious, but I don't think you are saying and I don't say you are thinking I don't think you are saying that these statements are in themselves meaningless?

JON

No—oh, good heavens, no. All I am saying really is that such statements are in themselves metaphysical statements.

ALAN

Metaphysical statements? Ah well, if they are metaphysical statements I do not think we should forget, or I don't think you should forget, as Bradley pointed out, that a man who rejects the existence of metaphysics is simply a metaphysician with a rival theory of his own. Oh dear, oh dear, oh dear.

JON

Yes, yes . . . ouch! In that case allow me to illustrate with an example from real life.

ALAN

You seem very fond of real life.

JON

Well, yes. Say we meet a friend say at the factory, or in the pub, or at the football match, we don't say to that friend, do we, Why are you? It would be quite absurd to say, Why are you?—no, we say, How are you?

ALAN

So we do. In this connection, what do you think of Plato and Aristotle and C. S. Lewis?

JON

Well, it seems to me that while Plato and Aristotle and C. S. Lewis—by the way, how is he?

ALAN

Oh, he's quite well.

35

JON

Oh, I am glad. Now, it seems to me while they had very interesting things to say about the society which they represent—

ALAN

He's been having a bit of bother with his teeth. They're not what they were.

JON

Oh, poor fellow.

ALAN

In fact, they're not where they were. They're out. It's a great loss to scholarship.

JON

Oh, I am sorry to hear that. But as I was saying, while these people—

ALAN

What people?

JON

Plato, Aristotle and poor old Toothless Lewis were asking questions about life and about death which are therefore entirely irrelevant.

ALAN

I call them not philosophers, but para-philosophers.

JON

Para-philosophers. How come para-philosophers?

ALAN

Well, you've heard of these chaps—paratroops—well, para-philosophers are the same, you see. Philosophers with their feet off the ground.

JON

Yes yes, very saucy. In that case, the burden is fair and square on your shoulders to explain to me the exact relevance philosophy does have on everyday life.

ALAN

Yes, I can do this quite easily. This morning I went into a shop, and a shop assistant was having an argument with a customer. The shop assistant said, "Yes," you see, and the customer said, "What do you mean, yes?" and the shop assistant said, "I mean yes."

JON

This is very exciting indeed.

ALAN

Here is a splendid example in everyday life where two very ordinary people are asking each other what are in essence philosophical questions—What do you mean, yes? —I mean yes—and where I, as a philosopher, could help them.

JON

And did you?

ALAN

Well, no—they were in rather a hurry—

Blackout

T.V.P.M.

PETER COOK SOLO

Good evening. I have recently been traveling round the world, on your behalf and at your expense, visiting some of the chaps with whom I hope to be shaping your future. I went first to Germany, and there I spoke with the German Foreign Minister, Herr . . . Herr and there. And we exchanged many frank words in our respective languages—

From thence I flew by Boeing to the Bahamas, where I was having talks with the American President, Mr. Kennedy, and I must say I was very struck by his youth and vigor. The talks we had were of a very friendly nature and at one time we even exchanged photographs of our respective families, and I was very touched, very touched indeed, to discover that here was yet another great world leader who regarded the business of Government as being a family affair.

Our talks ranged over a wide variety of subjects including that of the Skybolt Missile program. And after a great deal of good-natured give and take I decided on behalf of Great Britain to accept the Polaris in the place of the Skybolt. This is a good solution—as far as I can see, the Polaris starts where the Skybolt left off. In the sea.

I was privileged to see some actual photographs of this weapon. The President was kind enough to show me actual photographs of this missile, beautiful photographs taken by Karsch of Ottawa. A very handsome weapon, we shall be very proud to have them, the photographs, that is, we don't get the missiles till round about 1970—in the meantime we shall just have to keep our fingers crossed, sit very quietly and try not to alienate anyone.

This is not to say that we do not have our own Nuclear Striking Force—we do, we have the Blue Steel, a very effective missile, as it has a range of one hundred and fifty miles, which means we can just about get Paris—and by God we will.

While I was abroad I was very moved to receive letters from people in acute distress all over the country. And one in particular from an old-age pensioner in Fyfe is indelibly printed on my memory. Let me read it to you. It reads, "Dear Prime Minister, I am an old-age pensioner in Fyfe, living on a fixed income of some two pounds, seven shillings a week. This is not enough. What do you of the Conservative Party propose to do about it?"

(He tears up the letter)

Well, let me say right away, Mrs. MacFarlane—as one Scottish old-age pensioner to another—be of good cheer. There are many people in this country today who are far worse off than yourself. And it is the policy of the Conservative Party to see that this position is maintained.

And now I see the sands of time are alas drawing all too rapidly to a close, so I leave you all with that grand old Celtic saying that is so popular up there: good night, and may God be wi' ye!

Blackout

AND THE SAME TO YOU

DUDLEY MOORE SOLO

DUDLEY *plays this piece with touching solemnity—moving finally to the interminable coda, from which he extricates himself at the expense of his dignity and after an enormous amount of unnecessary effort.*

AFTERMYTH OF WAR

PETER

So you want to know about the war!

The thirties were coming to an end. Heavy with menace the forties were just around the corner. At the Victoria Palace, Lupino Lane was entrancing London with *Me and My Girl.*

At Ascot a year of Royal victories. Walt Disney had done it again with *Snow White and the Seven Dwarfs.*

JON

But underneath the gaiety, the storm clouds were gathering. Across Europe, German soldiers were dancing the hideous gavotte of war.

(PETER *and* ALAN *do a salute on the rostrum, then march down the steps*)

ALAN

And then came a break in the clouds.

(JON *comes through the arch with a paper bag. The others wave*)

JON

I have here from Herr Hitler a piece of paper.

(*The bang of the bursting paper bag is echoed by a tape of a bombing raid.* ALAN, *wearing a head scarf, steps onto the balcony*)

BEYOND THE FRINGE

ALAN

I'll always remember that weekend war broke out. I was at a house party at Cliveden with the Astors and we sat around listening to the moving broadcast by Mr. Churchill, or Mr. Chamberlain as he then was. I remember turning to my husband and saying, "Squiffy, où sont les neiges d'ans temps?" But I did not feel then that all was quite lost and immediately afterwards I got on the telephone to Berlin to try to speak to Herr Hitler, who had been so kind to us on our last visit to Germany that summer. Unfortunately the line was engaged. There was nothing I could do to avert the carnage of the next six years.

(Sound of explosion)

DUDLEY

Mr. Charles Spedding of Hoxton remembers:

PETER

(Coming up through the hatch)

I'll always remember the day that war was declared. I was out in the garden at the time, planting out some chrysanths. It was a grand year for chrysanths—1939, I wish we could have another one like it. My wife came out to me in the garden and told me about the outbreak of hostilities. "Never you mind," I says to her. "You put on the kettle, and we'll have a nice hot cup of tea."

(A siren shrieks)

DUDLEY

Put out that light. (PETER *goes* down *in the hatch*) All over Britain, the humble little people showed the same spirit of courage.

(JON *enters with a tea trolley, amidst the flashes and noise of an air raid*)

JON

You could always tell the difference between theirs and ours. Ours has a steady sort of reliable British hum, rather like a homely old bumblebee. Theirs, on the other hand, has a nasty intermittent whine rather like a ghastly foreign mosquito.

ALAN
(Off, on mike)

Meanwhile, as invasion threatened, England was blanketed in security.

(PETER *and* DUDLEY *enter with a signpost*)

PETER

Wait a moment now. We'll put Ipswich round there.

DUDLEY

We'll put Lyme Regis where Ipswich was.

PETER

And we'll put Great Yarmouth where Lyme Regis was. There now, that should fool the Boche. Bye-bye, then. Here —how do we get home?

JON

Home. The very word had a sort of comforting sound, didn't it? Homes whose very foundations were built upon the air. (PETER, ALAN *and* DUDLEY *pose on the steps*) Young men, scarcely boys, tossed aside youthful things and grew up overnight in the grimmer game that is war. A game where only one side was playing the game. Young men flocked to join the Few.

43

BEYOND THE FRINGE

DUDLEY

Please, sir, I want to join the Few.

JON

I'm sorry, there are far too many.

PETER

From the Rugby fields into the air.

JON

From the squash courts into the clouds.

ALAN

From the skiffs into the Spitfires.

JON

This was war.

ALAN

I had a pretty quiet war really. I was one of the Few. We were stationed down at Biggin Hill. One Sunday we got word Jerry was coming in. Over Broadstairs, I think it was. We got up there as quickly as we could, and you know, everything was very calm and peaceful. England lay like a green carpet below us, and the war seemed worlds away. I could see Tunbridge Wells and the sun glinting on the river, and I remembered that last weekend I spent there with Celia that summer of '39.

Suddenly, Jerry was coming at me out of a bank of cloud. I let him have it, and I think I must have got him in the wing because he spiraled past me out of control. As he did so—I will always remember this—I got a glimpse of his face, and you know—he smiled. Funny thing—war.

(*There is the sound of hearty singing.* PETER *enters on the rostrum*)

44

ALAN BENNETT, JONATHAN MILLER, DUDLEY MOORE and PETER COOK
in *"Aftermyth of War."*

DUDLEY MOORE, ALAN BENNETT, JONATHAN MILLER and PETER COOK
in *"So That's the Way You Like It."*

PETER

Perkins! Sorry to drag you away from the fun, old boy. War's not going very well, you know.

JON

Oh, my God!

PETER

We are two down, and the ball's in the enemy court. War is a psychological thing, Perkins, rather like a game of football. And you know how in a game of football ten men often play better than eleven—?

JON

Yes, sir.

PETER

Perkins, we are asking you to be that one man. I want you to lay down your life, Perkins. We need a futile gesture at this stage. It will raise the whole tone of the war. Get up in a crate, over to Bremen, take a shufti, don't come back. Good-bye, Perkins. God, I wish I was going too.

JON

Good-bye, sir—or perhaps it's *au revoir?*

PETER

No, Perkins.

(JON *exits*)

ALAN

But London, that gallant old lady, nurtures her children well.

BEYOND THE FRINGE

DUDLEY

At the National Gallery, in a series of lunchtime concerts, Dame Myra Hess wove her magic fingers inextricably into the heart strings of London.

ALAN

The music you are listening to, Timothy, is German music. We are fighting the Germans. That is something you are going to have to work out later on.

(*Gun shots intensify into an air raid.* JON *and* ALAN *crawl across the stage.* PETER *comes up through the trap*)

PETER

That was the night they got Pithy Street. I'll always remember it. I was out in the garden at the time planting out some deadly nightshade for the Boche. My wife came out to me in the garden and told me the abominable news: "Thousands have died in Pithy Street." "Never you mind the thousands of dead," I says to her. "You put on the kettle, we'll have a nice hot cup of tea!"

JON

How many children do you have, Andrews?

ALAN

Six, sir. How about you, sir?

JON

Mary and I only had twenty-four hours before I came out here. I've never even seen my son Timothy. We've got him down for Eton of course. He has the makings of a damn fine football player, Mary tells me.

BEYOND THE FRINGE

ALAN

Good show, sir.

JON

Andrews, I've not said this before, but we've been right through this beastly business together now, right the way through.

ALAN

So we have, sir.

JON

And until this horrible war started, I'd never known men of your class before, and there is just one thing I'd like to say, Andrews. It's been a privilege.

ALAN

God bless you, sir. God bless you.

JON

Right—this is it. Let's go.

DUDLEY

How grateful we were to the B.B.C. in those dark days of the war when every night at nine o'clock Alver Lidell brought us news of fresh disasters.

(*Sound of explosion*)

PETER

I never ever used to hear the nine o'clock news because I was always out in the garden round about nine-ish planting out some carrots for the night fighters. But I do remember that black, black day that rationing was imposed. My wife came out to me in the garden, her face a mask of pain.

47

"Charlie," she said, "rationing has been imposed and all that that entails." "Never mind, my dear," I says to her. "You put on the kettle—we'll have a nice cup of boiling hot water."

ALAN

But the tide was turning, the wicket was drying out. It was deuce, advantage Great Britain. Then America and Russia asked if they could join in and the whole thing turned into a free-for-all. So, unavoidably, came peace, putting an end to organized war as we knew it.

(*Flags fly, balloons fall, bells chime*)

PETER

Well, we've done our best, now it's up to the youngsters.

JON

I wonder what they'll make of it.

ALL

Should old acquaintance
Be forgot
And never brought to mind,
Should O . . . l . . . d A . . . c . . . q . . . u . . .
(ALL *droop*)

Curtain

Part Two

CIVIL WAR

ALAN *is sitting behind a table,* JON *and* PETER *on either side of him.*

ALAN

Her Britannic Majesty's Government is very anxious to popularize the notion of civil defense. Now, the Government's defense—what for want of a better word I'll call policy—is based on the concept of the deterrent. Say what for the purpose of argument I will call an unnamed power takes a nuclear missile and drops it on the United Kingdom. We in the United Kingdom would then take another nuclear missile and drop it on Russ . . . I mean the unnamed power. This, you see, would deter them from . . . no, well, it would effectively discourage them . . . well, it would jolly well serve them right. Now I have an apology to make to you. Tonight I was going to bring along a hydrogen bomb to show you—we do have one or two that we send round to women's institutes—that sort of thing. Unfortunately the one I had my eye on was being used this evening.

PETER

Now, a lot of people in this country today tend to think of the whole problem of the hydrogen bomb as being rather above their heads. Nothing could be further from the truth. The issue is a simple one—kill or be killed!

DUDLEY
(*In the audience*)

Or both! Ha ha.

PETER

I beg your pardon.

DUDLEY

I said, "Or both."

PETER

I thought you did. Thank you.

DUDLEY

Thank you.

PETER

Thank you.

DUDLEY

Not at all.

ALAN

Shut up.

PETER

Now, we shall receive four minutes' warning of any impending nuclear attack. Some people have said, "Oh, my goodness me—four minutes? That is not a very long time!" Well, I would remind those doubters that some people in this great country of ours can run a mile in four minutes. Basically, the defense of Great Britain rests in the hands of our Sea-slugs. If our Sea-slugs fail to get through, we shall fall back on our Blue-waters. If our Blue-waters let us down, we still have got good old germ warfare up our sleeves.

Thank goodness for that. Now I must admit here, that there is a very strong possibility that our Sea-slugs won't get through—the British Sea-slug is a ludicrously cumbersome vehicle depending as it does on a group of trained runners carrying it into enemy territory. Mind you, the boffins are working on it day and night, thinking of fitting it out with some ingenious device—wings or something—and turning it into some sort of flying machine, in which case it will be renamed Greased Lightning. I must sit down here, I can feel one of my spells coming on.

JON

So this does mean, if we are fortunate enough to be the aggressor, we are in a position to inflict a blow of twenty, thirty, or even forty mega-deaths—or to put that in more familiar terms, forty million lifeless forms strewn all about the place here and there. Jolly good. Following this, our Sea-slugs will then come into their own in a second wave, and bring our score up into the seventy- or even eighty-mega-death bracket, which is practically the maximum score permitted by the Geneva Convention.

ALAN

Now, one or two people are a wee bit worried in case somebody makes a boo-boo, presses the wrong button, and sends up one of these blessed missiles by mistake. Well, it could not happen. You see—before he presses that button he has to get on the telephone to Number 10 Downing Street, and say, "Now look, Mr. Macmillan, sir, can I press this button?" And Mr. Macmillan will say "Yes" or "No," as the mood takes him. Now, there is a flaw in this argument, and I can see one of you seem to have spotted it. What if Mr.

Macmillan is out? Perfectly simple—common sense, really—
they'd ask Lady Dorothy. Now, at this point I think I'll throw
the whole thing over to you. If you're at all worried about
civil defense, or have any questions you would like to ask
the panel, we'd be only too pleased to help. (DUDLEY *whistles,*
trying to attract their attention) Yes.

DUDLEY

Following the nuclear holocaust—could you tell me when
normal public services will be resumed?

JON

Very fair question. We have got it in hand of course.
Following Armageddon, we do hope to have public services
working fairly smoothly pretty soon after the event. Though
I feel, in all fairness, I should point out to all of you that it
must needs be something in the nature of a skeleton service.

PETER

What can we do from a practical point of view in the
event of a nuclear attack? Well, the first golden rule to
remember in hydrogen warfare is to be out of the area where
the attack is about to occur—get right out of the area because that's the danger area where the bombs are dropping.
Get right out of it—get right out of it— If you're out of it
you're well out of it, if you're in it you're really in it. If you
are caught in it when the missile explodes, for goodness' sake
don't move, stand absolutely stockstill—not under a tree, of
course—that could be extremely dangerous. Now—what about
radiation, I hear a strangled cry. Well, there is a lot you
can do about radiation as soon as the dust has settled—jump
into a brown paper bag. Draw it on rather like a shroud.
(ALAN *helps* PETER *into a brown paper bag*) It's perfectly
simple. You're very maneuverable. You can do anything

BEYOND THE FRINGE

you want to inside your bag! So there you have it. The bomb drops, the dust settles, jump into your brown paper bag, and hop along to your local civil defense leader.

ALAN

And he will tell you exactly where you can go.

Blackout

REAL CLASS

PETER

I think at about this juncture it would be wise to point out to those of you who haven't noticed—and God knows it's apparent enough—that Jonathan Miller and myself come from good families and have had the benefits of a public-school education. Whereas the other two members of the cast have worked their way up from working-class backgrounds. Yet Jonathan and I are working together with them and treating them as equals, and I must say it's proving to be a most worthwhile, enjoyable and stimulating experience for both of us. Wouldn't you agree, Jonathan?

JON

Oh yes, extremely so. Very stimulating.

ALAN

Well, I suppose we are working class. But I wonder how many of those people realize that Jonathan Miller is a Jew.

DUDLEY

Yes—well, he is a Jew but one of the better sort.

ALAN

I would rather be working class than a Jew.

BEYOND THE FRINGE

DUDLEY

Good Lord, yes—there's no comparison, is there? But think of the awful situation if you were working class and a Jew.

ALAN

There is always someone worse off than yourself.

JON

In fact, I'm not really a Jew. Just Jewish.

Blackout

LITTLE MISS BRITTEN

JON

Dudley Moore continues to accompany himself on the pianoforte, this time in settings of English songs. A setting by Benjamin Britten of the old English air, "Little Miss Muffet." The "Little Miss Muffet" referred to is thought to have been related to the English entomologist of the same name.

(JON *exits*)

DUDLEY
(*Playing and singing*)

Little Miss Muffet
Sat on a tuffet
Eating her curds
Eating her curds
Eating her curds and whey.
There came a big spider
And sat down beside her
And frightened Miss Muffet
Away
Away
Away
Away
And frightened Miss Muffet away.
(*He ends with a crashing chord*)

Blackout

THE SUSPENSE IS KILLING ME

PETER *stands upstage holding a notice: "A Death Cell."*
PETER *exits.*
DUDLEY *and* JON *sit downstage, playing chess.*

DUDLEY

There we are, sir. Your move. Oh, I do believe I've got
your bishop there.

JON

Is it going to hurt?

DUDLEY

Look. I wouldn't worry about that if I was you, sir. You
take a tip from me, I've seen hundreds come and go—relax,
let yourself go loose. You're in experienced hands—he's a
craftsman, sir.

JON

Is it going to hurt?

DUDLEY

Well, I suppose it's rather like a visit to the dentist. It's
always worse in anticipation. But you won't see any of the
apparatus if that's what you are worried about—you'll have
a little white bag over your head.

JON

What white bag?

DUDLEY

It's just a little white bag, sir. They make them in Birmingham. But I can't explain to you what goes on out there, I'm not here for that sort of thing—am I now? You wait till the prison governor comes down—he'll set your mind at rest. Really he will.

(ALAN *enters*)

ALAN

'Morning, and a lovely morning it is too. Though there will be rain before the day is out. Fine before eleven, rain before seven. You know what they say.

DUDLEY

So you'll be missing the rain, sir, won't you?

ALAN

I don't mind saying, you know, there's been an awful hoo-ha in Parliament about you, and so far as I can see, the Home Secretary doesn't like this business any more than you do. But you know what parliamentary procedure is, and the case being sub-judice and all that—anyway, we'll see if we can't do something about it afterwards. You know, when I was at school I was a bit of a lad, and whenever I used to get into a scrape my headmaster used to say to me, "Now look here, I'll give you a choice, you can either be gated for a fortnight, or you can take six of the best and we'll forget all about it!" Well, like any self-respecting lad I used to take six of the best—what's the difference between this and capital punishment? You don't want to be cooped up for life.

JON

Yes, I do want to be cooped up for life.

ALAN

Come along, now, you're playing with words.
(*A bell starts tolling.* JON *and* ALAN *exit up the stairs. There is a great sound of bells, then a CRASH offstage*)

PETER
(*Re-entering in the silence*)

I think it should be done in public.

Blackout

PORN SHOPPING

JONATHAN MILLER SOLO

Some years ago when I was a medical student I became rather interested in the shops that one finds down the Charing Cross Road in London.

THE SHOPS . . .

where for some curious reason rupture appliances and trusses seem to feature rather prominently.

NOW . . .

I've often wondered to myself why it was that these forms of surgical apparatus did feature in these shops and thought that perhaps it might be some indication of the amount of strenuousness of the life led in the Charing Cross Road and its environments.

I also became interested in the books which they have on sale alongside the trusses in these shops.

NOW . . .

the sort of books I had in mind are not the sort of book that one can look at *directly* in the windows of the shops concerned.

THEY ARE . . .

the sort of book that one has to glance at "en passant" as one goes down the Charing Cross Road— HmmmHM-MMM—!

BEYOND THE FRINGE

I decided to do a sort of sociological survey on the sort of people that bought these books.

SO . . .

one day I took the bull by the horns and entered one of these shops and I found inside a fantastic jungle foliage of rupture appliances and trusses and varicose-vein bandages and all manner of surgically restraining devices of one sort or another and rejuvenating instruments of very sinister shapes and designs all hanging from the ceiling like tropical creepers.

SO . . .

I hacked my way to the back, where I found the proprietor of the shop hanging like an ancient orangutan from one of his own trusses . . . so I taxed him directly.

I SAID . . .

Now look, who buys all these books which you have on sale in the window here. And he said, Well, it's mainly for young married couples wanting to know your wherefore and why.

AND I SAID . . .

Well yes, I can understand your young married couples wanting to buy books like *Sexual Hygiene in Marriage* but surely your young married couples don't really buy books like a history of flogging in the Army, Navy and Air Force.

AND HE AGREED
WITH ME . . .

that by and large young married couples didn't buy that sort of book in bulk at any rate although a history of the thumbscrew in the home counties had a certain limited sale which I suppose is understandable.

AND SO . . .

I said, Well then, who do buy these books? And he said . . . Well, I suppose you might call them a more mature class of person, sir. Now this mature class of which I glibly speak falls into what I might best describe as your two broad categ'ries, sir.

TWO VERY BROAD
CATEG'RIES

On the one hand, there's your medical students like yourself . . . After all, perversions are in your curriculum, aren't they, sir?

AND . . .

on the other hand, by far the largest categ'ry I'm sorry to say, sir, is your straight warped! It's your straight warped types that walks in here and asks for books on flogging and the like . . . and if you want my opinion, sir, there's only one cure for that class of warped, distorted mind.

SO I LEANED FORWARD . . . anxious to hear of fresh developments in psychotherapy in this area and he said:

Yeah, there's only one cure for them, sir. It's a sock in the face and a kick in the arse and whip 'em to death, sir. Yeah, take a whip to them, sir. Give 'em a good dose of their own medicine . . . Yeaaaggghhh.

Blackout

STUDIO 5

This week Studio 5 welcomes three distinguished visitors. Now, Mr. Taylor, as a member of the campaign for nuclear disarmament, how do you feel about the Labour Party decision to reject nuclear disarmament?

ALAN

Well, frankly I am a little disappointed, but I know it does not represent the opinion of the rank and file of the Labour Party.

PETER

How do you come to this conclusion, Mr. Taylor?

ALAN

All I can say is this. We sent round a referendum to all our local branches phrased in this form: Would you like to see your wife and kids go up in smoke? Ninety-four per cent of the replies said *No*. If that is not a mandate for unilateral nuclear disarmament I do not know what is.

PETER

Mr. Taylor, thank you. We have with us this evening the newly appointed Lord Chamberlain. Lord Cobbold, what is your opinion of censorship in the theatre?

DUDLEY

Censorship in the theatre. Well, frankly I feel there's far too much sex and violence gets by in the name of entertainment these days. I mean, I go to the theatre to be entertained, I want to be taken out of myself. I don't want to see lust and rape, incest and sodomy—I can get all that at home.

PETER

Also with us this evening we have Mr. Andake Nobitsu, the leader of the Pan-African Federal Party, who is over here for the African Constitutional Conference. Now, Mr. Nobitsu, what hopes do you hold out for a successful conclusion to this conference?

JON

There can be no hope for a successful conclusion to this conference, until the fundamental rights of man are realized by the British Government. One man, one vote. That is the law of God which all must obey, including God. One man, one vote, that is essential—especially for the nine million black idiots who vote for me.

PETER

Mr. Nobitsu, how do you view the imprisonment of your colleague Mr. Bandabaku?

JON

The imprisonment of Mr. Bandabaku is a most immoral, disgusting, illegal and despicable act. And I am in favor of it as it lets me get on with a little bit of agitating on my own.

BEYOND THE FRINGE

Do you in any way condone the violent methods adopted by some members of your party to further their cause?

JON

By violent methods, Mr. Edwards, I presume you are referring to the isolated and sporadic outbreaks of entire communities being wiped out?

PETER

Yes, I did have that in mind.

JON

Well, all I can say to that is "Mote and beam."

PETER

I beg your pardon.

JON

"Mote and beam."

PETER

Mote and beam?

JON

"Mote and beam." Wipe out the mote from your own eye, Great Britain, before you start messing about with our beams. Everywhere the black man is misrepresented. For example, recently I went to see this play in London, "Fings Ain't What They Used To Be," and in this play there was a black man who was laying about all over the stage doing nothing, implying that all black men are layabouts.

PETER

But surely, Mr. Nobitsu, you might as well say the same play implies that all white people were pimps or prostitutes.

JON

Well, that is fair comment. There can be no progress, Mr. Edwards, until you Englishmen stop looking down your noses at us Africans.

PETER

Yes, I think I see what you mean.

JON

Black equals white, Mr. Edwards, no taxation without representation. Black equals white.

PETER

Mr. Nobitsu, one thing rather puzzles me—your hair is extremely straight, and your complexion seems to be white in color.

JON

That is perfectly true. I have recently undergone an operation to straighten my hair and also to remove the pigmentation from my skin.

PETER

Doesn't this rather fly in the face of all your principles?

JON

Not at all. I feel in this way I can represent the interests of my people best by speaking to the white man on his own

ground. Besides, it is the only way in which I can get lodg-
ings!

PETER

Mr. Nobitsu, thank you, and good night ... There, I
think we are safe now. If you would like to go up and join
Lord Cobbold and Mr. Taylor, I'm sure you three must have
lots to talk about.

(PETER *exits.* JON *joins* ALAN *and* DUDLEY *on the rostrum.
They stand in embarrassed silence*)

Blackout

SITTING ON THE BENCH

This piece was largely improvised and was changed nightly.

PETER COOK SOLO

Yes, I could have been a judge but I never had the Latin,
never had the Latin for the judging, I just never had suffi-
cient of it to get through the rigorous judging exams. They're
noted for their rigor. People come staggering out saying, "My
God, what a rigorous exam—" And so I became a miner
instead. A coal miner. I managed to get through the mining
exams—they're not very rigorous, they only ask you one
question, they say "Who are you?" and I got seventy-five per
cent on that—

Of course, it's quite interesting work, getting hold of
lumps of coal all day, it's quite interesting. Because the coal
was made in a very unusual way. You see, God blew all the
trees down. He didn't just say let's have some coal. As He
could have done, He had all the right contacts. No, He got
this great wind going, you see, and blew down all the trees,
then, over a period of three million years, He changed it into
coal, gradually over a period of three million years so it
wasn't noticeable to the average passer-by. It was all part of
the scheme, but people at the time did not see it that way.
People under the trees did not say, "Hurrah—coal in three
million years," no, they said, "Oh dear, oh dear, trees falling
on us—that's the last thing we want," and of course their
wish was granted.

70

I am very interested in the universe—I am specializing in the universe and all that surrounds it. I am studying Nesbitt's book—*The Universe and All That Surrounds It, an introduction*. He tackles the subject boldly, goes from the beginning of time right through to the present day, which according to Nesbitt is October 31, 1940. And he says the earth is spinning into the sun and we will all be burnt to death. But he ends the book on a note of hope, he says, "I hope this will not happen." But there's not a lot of interest in this down the mine.

The trouble with it is the people. I am not saying you get a load of riffraff down the mine, I am not saying that, I am just saying we had a load of riffraff down my mine. Very boring conversationalists, extremely boring, all they talk about is what goes on in the mine. Extremely boring. If you were searching for a word to describe the conversations that go on down the mine, boring would spring to your lips. —Oh God! They're very boring. If ever you want to hear things like: "Hello, I've found a bit of coal. Have you really? Yes, no doubt about it, this black substance is coal all right. Jolly good, the very thing we're looking for." It is not enough to keep the mind alive, is it?

Whoops. Did you notice I suddenly went *whoops?* It's an impediment I got from being down the mine. 'Cause one day I was walking along in the dark when I came across the body of a dead pit pony. Whoops, I went in surprise, and ever since then I've been going *whoops* and that's another reason I couldn't be a judge, because I might have been up there all regal, sentencing away, "I sentence you to *whoops,*" and you see, the trouble is under English law that would have to stand. So all in all I'd rather have been a judge than a miner.

And what is more, being a miner, as soon as you are too old and tired and sick and stupid to do the job properly, you have to go. Well, the very opposite applies with the judges. So all in all I would rather have been a judge than a miner—

Because I've always been after the trappings of great luxury you see, I really, really have. But all I've got hold of are the trappings of great poverty. I've got hold of the wrong load of trappings, and a rotten load of trappings they are too, ones I could've very well done without.

Blackout

BREAD ALONE

JON

Very good to see you.

ALL

Very good to see you. Nice to see you.

ALAN

Unless I'm very much mistaken, there's the bar.

JON

Magic words bar, ha, ha, ha.

ALL

Here we are and there we are. Ahhhh, ahh. Yes, yes.

ALAN

Ay, ay, ay.

ALL

Ay, ay, ay.
                (There is a brief period of noises)

ALAN

Funny old world.

73

ALL

Funny old world.

PETER

Well, what are you going to have?

ALL

Let me get this one. My round. I insist, my round! What are you going to have?

PETER

Large whiskey.

JON

Double brandy.

DUDLEY

Glass of vino tinty.

ALAN

Rosé.

ALL

Right. I'll get this. No, I insist, this one's on me. Drinks are on me. Drinks on me.
(*There is a general search for money, with accompanying noises*)

JON

I've got nothing on me.

ALL

I'm cleaned out. Haven't got a thing on me. Not a penny.

DUDLEY

Do they take luncheon vouchers?

PETER

Have you got one?

DUDLEY

No.

PETER

Well, they don't take them unless you actually have one.

JON

Now, where are we going to sit for lunch?

ALL

I don't mind. I'm quite immaterial. I don't mind.

PETER

This is the only table here.
(*After another period of noises, they sit down at the table*)

ALL

Well, let's sit over there.

JON

Let's get hold of the waiter.

ALL

Waiter! Waiter!

JON

I've got one. Jolly good. Now what are we going to have?

ALL

Aaahhhhhhh.

PETER

It all looks jolly good to me.

JON

I'll have the same as you.

PETER

Same as me, eh—I'll go along with you, Buffy, you know this place best.

JON

Stop smelling your menu and order, Buffy.

ALAN

Buffy, come on.

DUDLEY

I'm not smelling the menu, I can't see a thing. Think I've got my contact lenses in back to front.

ALAN
(*Holding up the menu*)

Try this, Buffy.

DUDLEY
(*Reading the list of appetizers*)

Oh, I can't decide. I'll follow you, Squiff.

ALAN

I decided long ago, I'm having what you're having.

JON

Good. That's four of the same. Where's he gone? Bloody waiter's cleared off. Go find him, Squiff.

ALAN

All right. Waiter!

(ALAN *exits*)

THREE

That's it—gone. Cleared off. Bloody waiter's cleared off. I always come here and it is always the same. Didn't I tell you?

Blackout

TAKE A PEW

ALAN BENNETT SOLO

The eleventh verse of the twenty-seventh chapter of the book of Genesis, "But my brother Esau is an hairy man, but I am a smooth man"—"my brother Esau is an hairy man, but I am a smooth man." Perhaps I can paraphrase this, say the same thing in a different way by quoting you some words from the grand old prophet, Nehemiah, Nehemiah seven, sixteen.

And he said unto me, what seest thou
And I said unto him, lo
        (*He reads the next four lines twice*)
I see the children of Bebai,
Numbering six hundred and seventy-three,
And I see the children of Asgad
Numbering one thousand, four hundred and seventy-four.

There come times in the lives of each and every one of us when we turn aside from our fellows and seek the solitude and tranquillity of our own firesides. When we put up our feet and put on our slippers, and sit and stare into the fire. I wonder at such times whether your thoughts turn, as mine do, to those words I've just read you now.

They are very unique and very special words, words that express as so very few words do that sense of lack that lies at the very heart of modern existence. That I - don't - quite - know - what - it - is - but - I'm - not - getting - everything - out - of - life - that - I - should - be - getting sort of feeling. But they are more than this, these words, much, much more—they are in a very real sense a challenge to each and every one of us here tonight. What is that challenge?

As I was on my way here tonight, I arrived at the station, and by an oversight I happened to come out by the way one is supposed to go in, and as I was coming out an employee of the railway company hailed me. "Hey, mate," he shouted, "where do you think you are going?" That at any rate was the gist of what he said. You know, I was grateful to him, because, you see, he put me in mind of the kind of question I felt I ought to be asking you here tonight. Where do you think you're going?

Very many years ago when I was about as old as some of you are now, I went mountain climbing in Scotland with a very dear friend of mine. And there was this mountain, you see, and we decided to climb it. And so, very early one morning, we arose and began to climb. All day we climbed. Up and up and up. Higher and higher and higher. Till the valley lay very small below us, and the mists of the evening began to come down, and the sun to set. And when we reached the summit we sat down to watch this most magnificent sight of the sun going down behind the mountain. And as we watched, my friend very suddenly and violently vomited.

Some of us think Life's a bit like that, don't we? But it isn't. You know, Life—Life, it's rather like opening a tin of sardines. We are all of us looking for the key. Some of us—some of us think we've found the key, don't we? We roll back the lid of the sardine tin of Life, we reveal the sardines, the riches of Life, therein and we get them out, we enjoy them. But, you know, there's always a little piece in the corner you can't get out. I wonder—I wonder, is there a little piece in the corner of your life? I know there is in mine.

So now I draw to a close. I want you when you go out into the world, in times of trouble and sorrow and helplessness and despair amid the hurly-burly of modern life, if ever you're tempted to say, "Oh, shove this!" I want you then to remember, for comfort, the words of my first text to you tonight . . .

"But my brother Esau is an hairy man,
    but I am a smooth man."

Blackout

SO THAT'S THE WAY YOU LIKE IT

PETER

Sustain we now description of a time
When petty lust and overweening tyranny
Offend the ruck of state.
Thus fly we now, as oft with Phoebus did
Fair Asterope unto proud Flander's court.
Where is the warlike Warwick
Like to the mole that sat on Hector's brow,
Fairset for England, and for war!
(JON and ALAN enter)

JON

And so we bid you welcome to our court,
Fair cousin Albany, and you, our sweetest Essex,
Take this my hand, and you, fair Essex, this,
And with this bond we'll cry anon
And shout Jack Cock of London to the foe.
Approach your ears and kindly bend your conscience to my
                                                      piece,
Our ruddy scouts to me this hefty news have brought:
The naughty English, expecting now some pregnance in our
                                                      plan,
Have with some haughty purpose
Bent Aeolis unto the service of their sail.
So even now while we to the wanton lute do strut

Is brutish Bolingbroke bent fair upon
Some fickle circumstance.

ALAN and PETER

Some fickle circumstance!

JON

Get thee to Gloucester, Essex. Do thee to Wessex, Exeter.
Fair Albany to Somerset must eke his route.
And Scroup, do you to Westmoreland, where shall bold York
Enrouted now for Lancaster, with forces of our uncle Rutland,
Enjoin his standard with sweet Norfolk's host.
Fair Sussex, get thee to Warwicksbourne,
And there, with frowning purpose, tell our plan
To Bedford's tilted ear, that he shall press
With most insensate speed
And join his warlike effort to bold Dorset's side.
I most royally shall now to bed,
To sleep off all the nonsense I've just said.
(*They exit.* ALL *re-enter*)

JON

Is it botched up then, Master Puke?

ALAN

Aye, marry and is, good Master Snot.

DUDLEY

'Tis said our Master, the Duke, hath contrived some naughtiness against his son, the King.

PETER

Aye, and it doth confound our merrymaking.

JON

What say you, Master Puke? I am for Lancaster, and that's to say for good shoe leather.

PETER

Come speak, good Master Puke, or hath the leather blocked up thy tongue?

DUDLEY

Why then go trippingly upon thy laces, good Grit.

PETER

Art leather laces thy undoing?

DUDLEY

They shall undo many a fair boot this day.

ALL

Come. Let's to our rural revel and with our song enchant our King.

(ALL *exit.* ALAN *and* DUDLEY *re-enter*)

DUDLEY
(*Sings*)

Oh, Death, his face my shroud hath hid
And Lethe drowned my poor love's soul,
So flee we now to Pluto's realm
And in his arms shall I grow old.

ALAN

Wise words in mouths of fools do oft themselves belie. Good fool—shall Essex prosper?

BEYOND THE FRINGE

DUDLEY

Aye, prosper.

ALAN

Say you—prosper, fool?

DUDLEY

Aye, prosper.

ALAN

Marry then, methinks we'll prosper. And saying prosper, do we say to cut the knot which crafty nature hath within our bowels locked up. But soft and who comes here?

(PETER *enters*)

PETER

Oh good my Lord, unstop your ear and yet
Prepare to yield the optic tear to my experience,
Such news I bring as only can crack ope
The casket of thy soul.
Not six miles hence
There grows an oak whose knotty thews
Engendered in the bosky wood doth raise itself
Most impudent towards the solstice sun—
So saying did there die and dying so did say.

ALAN

God! this was most gravely underta'en
And underta'en hath Essex gravely answered it.
Why then we'll muster and to the field of battle go
And unto them our English sinews show.

(ALL *exit. Smoke swirls about the stage.* PETER *and* JON *enter with swords*)

84

JON

Why then was this encounter nobly entertained
And so by steel shall this our contest now be buckled up.
Come, sir. Let's to it.

PETER

Let's to it.
Good steel, thou shalt thyself in himself thyself embowel.

JON

Come, sir. (*They fight*) Ah ha, a hit!

PETER

No, sir, no hit, a miss! Come, sir, art foppish i' the mouth.

JON

Art more fop in the mouth than fop in the steel.
(*They fight again.* PETER *"hits"* JON)

JON

Oh God, fair cousin, thou hast done me wrong.
(*He "dies"*)
Now is steel twixt gut and bladder interposed.

PETER

Oh, saucy Worcester, dost thou lie so still?
(ALAN *enters*)

ALAN

Now hath mortality her tithe collected.
And sovereign Albany to the worms his course committed.
Yet weep we not; this fustian life is short,
Let's on to Pontefract to sanctify our court.

Blackout

THE END OF THE WORLD

How will it be, this end of which you have spoken, Brother Enim?

ALL

Yes, how will it be?

PETER

Well, it will be as it t'were a mighty rending in the sky, and the mountains will sink, and the valleys will rise and great will be the tumult thereof.

JON

Will the vale of the temple be rent in twain?

PETER

It will be rent in twain about two minutes before we see the manifest flying beast head in the sky.

ALAN

And will there be a mighty wind?

PETER

Certainly there will be a mighty wind, if the word of God is anything to go by.

DUDLEY

And will this wind be so mighty as to lay low the mountains of the earth?

PETER

No. It will not be quite as mighty as that. That is why we have come up on the mountain, you stupid nit. To be safe from it.

JON

All right then—when will it be?

ALL

Ah, when will it be?

PETER

In about thirty seconds' time, according to the ancient pyramidic scrolls.

JON

Shall we compose ourselves then?

PETER

Good plan. Prepare for the end of the world. Fifteen seconds!

DUDLEY

Here, have you got the picnic basket?

ALAN

Yes.

PETER

Five, four, three, two, one, zero!

ALL

Now is the end,
Perish the world!

PETER

It was G.M.T., wasn't it?

JON

Yes.

PETER

Well, it's not quite the conflagration we'd been banking on.
Never mind, lads, same time tomorrow, we must get a win-
ner one day.

Curtain